# STABILIZE PROTECT AMPLIFY

## Using legal strategy to build a business that rocks!

## JOLEEN WINTHER HUGHES

# CONTENTS

# Testimonials

*"A must-read playbook for turning big ideas into unstoppable momentum. Sharp, inspiring, and impossible to put down." – Misha Lyalin, ZeptoLab*

*"Joleen has an incredible gift for translating complex legal concepts into practical, bite-sized wisdom. 'Stabilize. Protect. Amplify.' is not just a legal guide—it's a playbook every creative entrepreneur should have. The music-industry analogies are not only clever but also make the content engaging and memorable. I walked away with actionable tips I could use immediately. Highly recommend!" – Aisha Martin, Founder, CEO of Aisha Hopkins Management*

*" Having built and led a business for over 20 years, I've read my share of legal and business guides. Stabilize. Protect. Amplify. stands out for its clarity and practicality. We've valued Joleen's legal counsel over the years, not only*

*for her expertise in the law, but also for her creativity and understanding of what it takes to run and grow a successful company. This book reflects that rare combination. It is a thoughtful, actionable resource for entrepreneurs who want to build with intention and navigate growth with confidence." – Colleen Alderman, Founding Partner, Communique PR*

*"Joleen Winther Hughes brings street-smart business savvy from rock and roll and digital media to deliver essential business legal strategies. Stabilize, Protect and Amplify is your definitive set list for success - straight from the lawyer who rocks!" – Virl Hill, Board of Directors, SIFF.net*

*"Sometimes, it's important for a business to go a little slow to go faster later. As every serial entrepreneur knows (mostly from our mistakes), this is especially true when setting up a company and establishing the foundational templates like customer contracts and employee agreements. Stabilize. Protect. Amplify. is the perfect primer for first-time founders as well as a great reminder when starting your nth company. It is the framework for a productive conversation with your legal team to cover the most critical topics. Set your legal guardrails early and ensure your business*

can accelerate quickly." – Marty Roberts, COO, Tagboard, Inc.

"Joleen has created something special with 'Stabilize, Protect, Amplify.' The use of music metaphors throughout—from 'tuning up' your business foundation to avoiding legal 'feedback'—makes complex legal concepts not only accessible but actually engaging. I appreciated how the information flowed when framed through the lens of building a band and creating great music.

What really works for me is how years of legal expertise is translated into practical, actionable advice that any business owner can understand and use. She doesn't just tell you what to do—she explains why it matters and how each piece fits into your overall business strategy. The 'backstage pass' approach makes you feel like you're getting some inside scoop from someone who truly understands the legal and creative sides of business.

This can be a useful roadmap that can be referenced again and again as the business grows. An easy and enjoyable read with lots of useful information. " – Shelia Rue, VP Customer Experience

*"I can't believe I started a business without this quick read of a book. No wonder I made so many costly mistakes!"* – Lisa Strain, CEO, Kari Gran Inc.

**This book is for:**

My husband, Gareth, thank you for always having a firm grip on my hand when we leap. Your belief makes the impossible feel inevitable.

Our clients, your trust means everything. You push us to lead with clarity, own our role, and stay sharp in every room we walk into.

# DISCLAIMER

THE INFORMATION PROVIDED IN this book is for general informational purposes only and does not constitute legal advice.

Lawyers are ethically obligated to provide advice that is tailored to the nuances of each client's situation, which cannot be achieved through generalized information alone.

Every business is unique, and the legal needs of your business may vary based on specific facts, circumstances, and jurisdictions.

For advice that is specific to your business, consult a qualified attorney. If you are interested in setting up a consultation with Hughes Media Law Group, please visit hmlglaw.com or scan the QR code.

To the maximum extent provided by law, Hughes Media Law Group, the author and publisher disclaim any liability for actions taken or not taken based on the contents of this book without seeking the advice of an attorney.

# Introduction
## Why This Isn't Just Another Business Guide

EVERY GREAT BAND STARTS with a dream, a gritty riff, a lightning lyric, or a sound so raw and alive it stops people in their tracks. Magic happens when instinct meets intention.

Before I ever practiced law, I was chasing that same magic, only I found it in business.

During the 90s, while Seattle's music scene exploded, I was right there with it. I managed bands, booked shows, ran a production company, and built a business during a time when deals were made with handshakes and duct tape. I didn't have a law degree. I had hustle, intuition, and the ability to get things done.

Eventually, I went to law school. I thought adding legal expertise to my street smarts would round out my experience. What I didn't expect was how disconnected most lawyers were from the real world. Once I joined one of the most forward-thinking tech companies on the planet as in-house counsel, I hired every type of law firm you can imagine, from towering skyscrapers of Big Law to niche boutiques. What I discovered was eye-opening.

Most of them had never run a business. Never negotiated under pressure. Never had to make a decision with both their wallet and their integrity on the line. They gave advice from the sidelines and didn't understand the rhythm of the game.

That's when I knew: my dual path, hustling in the real world, then learning how to protect and scale those ideas legally, wasn't just unique. It was powerful.

So I built a law firm around it.

I didn't want to create a traditional practice. I wanted to create a space where lawyers were part of the band, not just roadies behind the scenes. Where legal counsel didn't slow a business down but helped it rise, evolve, and perform on bigger stages.

This guide is part of that mission. Think of it as your legal soundcheck, a backstage pass to ideas that help your business stay in tune, hit every note, and keep the lights on for the encore.

You won't find fear-based legal lectures here. You won't find hollow hype, either.

You'll find real insights drawn from decades of navigating the crossroads of creativity, risk, and growth.

Consider this your backstage pass. With a few foundational tools and smart moves, your business can stay sharp, agile, and performance-ready.

Are you ready?

Great! Let's crank the volume.

# 1
# TUNE UP
## Entity Formation for a Stable Foundation

WHEN I MANAGED BANDS, I learned one thing fast: if you don't have the right foundation, everything can fall apart.

The same goes for your business. Entity formation and governance aren't merely legal formalities, they're the stage you build to stabilize everything else.

Unfortunately, I've seen too many entrepreneurs skimp on this step, only to face costly consequences later.

Without the right entity structure, you could:

- **Pay 2-3 Times More to Fix It**: Untangling a poorly set-up business can cost significantly more in legal fees than doing it right the first time.

- **Lose Equity or Control**: If corporate paperwork isn't done properly, people can come out of the woodwork claiming ownership, leaving you fighting to protect what's yours.

- **Miss Out on Opportunities**: Investors won't touch a business with messy or incomplete legal foundations, leaving you stuck without the capital to grow.

Whether you're a startup dreaming big or an established business ready to scale, your entity is the foundation to stabilize your company and the first step to ensure long-term success.

## Why a Stable Foundation Rocks

Your business structure sets the tone for everything that follows. Here's why paying attention to the details is non-negotiable:

- **Protect Your Personal Assets**: Without the right structure, your personal wealth is on the line if things go south.

- **Unlock Tax Advantages**: The right entity can save you thousands (or more) in taxes.

- **Build Credibility**: Investors, partners, and clients take you more seriously when you pay attention to the details.

- **Prepare for Growth**: A stable foundation

makes it easier to raise capital, form partnerships, and scale.

**_Pro Tip_**: Every state has one or more statutes which are the default rules governing business entities. By customizing your operating agreement, bylaws, or shareholder agreements, you can operate your business the way you desire, not the way the state dictates.

## The Pitfalls of DIY Legal Documentation

Using services like LegalZoom or AI to prepare your paperwork might seem like an easy way to save money in the early stages of your company. But, trust me, you get what you pay for.

Entity formation isn't merely about checking boxes or spitting out some generic shareholder agreement. It's about understanding how your structure impacts everything from taxes to liability to future growth, and realizing you have control over how you run the business.

Companies who use DIY legal docs for their formation often realize later they've chosen the wrong structure, missed key tax benefits, or left themselves exposed to unnecessary risks by failing to have the correct documentation in place.

Make no mistake, fixing is _always_ more expensive than getting it right the first time.

## Stabilize Your Business: Key Steps to Set Yourself Up for Success

### 1. Choose the Right Structure.

Each business structure comes with its own pros and cons and must comply with the specific laws of the state it is filed in. The right choice of entity depends on your goals, industry, and growth plans:

- **Limited Liability Company (LLC).** A pass-through legal entity made up of members or managers. Great for protecting personal assets and is extremely flexible. Governed by an Operating Agreement. Members are subject to self-employment taxes.

- **C-Corporation (C-Corp).** The default corporate legal entity made up of a board, officers, and owned by unlimited shareholders. Subject to corporate tax rate. Multiple classes of stock. Governed by the shareholder agreement and company by-laws. Ideal if you want to separate ownership vs. control of the company and give yourself more flexibility to raise capital or go public.

- **S-Corporation (S-Corp)**. A pass-through elective corporate entity made up of a board, officers and owned by 100 or fewer shareholders, who must be U.S. citizens or permanent residents. One class of stock. Governed by the shareholder agreement and company by-laws.

- **Social Purpose Corporations (SPC) or Flexible Purpose Corporations (FPC).** Each is a type of for-profit corporation which enables a company to identify a legitimate corporate purpose beyond maximizing shareholder value. For example: considering social or environmental issues in decision making. Additional compliance requirements and tax considerations may apply. Not available in every state.

- **B-Corporation (B-Corp).** A variation of the C-Corp which requires a report to indicate what efforts the company has made to create a public benefit for "stakeholders" rather than shareholders. Stakeholders may not be shareholders.

- **Non-Profit Organizations**. Entities which focus on social and charitable goals and require a more extensive governance and infrastructure to maintain their tax status.

## 2. Governance

Good governance isn't just about compliance, it's about creating a framework for success. Depending on which entity you choose, make sure you implement:

- **Correct Paperwork**. Make sure you have state-specific written operating documents which are specific to your selected type of entity. Some entities have additional requirements on a state-by-state basis.

- **Local, State, and Federal Filings**. Ensure you obtain proper tax identification numbers, file for necessary business licenses, set up accounts with local offices (e.g. sales tax).

- **Board and Shareholder Meetings**: Follow your company documentation to ensure you're complying with legal requirements like holding regular governance meetings and keeping records.

- **Director and Officer Agreements**: Execute agreements with your board of directors and officers to clearly define roles and responsibilities.

- **Standardized Policies and Procedures**: Develop policies and operational procedures to standardize your operations.

## 3. Plan for the Future

Your entity structure should support your long-term vision, whether you're planning on maintaining a small business, building a lasting empire or scaling rapidly for a quick exit. Start as you mean to finish using three imperative tools:

- **Cap Table**: Keep your equity structure updated, clear and organized to avoid headaches during fundraising or exits.

- **Equity and Incentive Plans**: Attract and retain top talent with well-designed equity and incentive plans.

- **Succession Planning**: Plan for a time when you won't be there to run the business. Whether you're selling, going public, or passing the business to the next generation, your entity structure should support your goals.

## 4. Beyond Formation

A well-structured entity makes your business more attractive to investors, buyers, or partners. Once your entity is set up, however, the foundational work isn't over if you want to maintain long-term success.

- **Due Diligence:** Continuously and proactively vet your business to identify strengths, weaknesses, and potential deal-breakers.

- **Streamlined Processes**: Keep your records organized. Implement clear governance and document policies so everyone operates from the same set of rules.

- **Integration Planning**: Ensure a seamless transition after a merger or acquisition.

## The Final Chord

A band needs the right gear as a foundation to deliver an unforgettable performance. Likewise, your business needs the right legal setup to support growth, protect your assets, and keep everything in harmony.

Dial it in early and you'll be free to focus on what matters, creating something that truly rocks.

# NOTES

DATE: _____________

# 2
# FORMING THE BAND
## Who's Backing You Up?

A BAND IS ONLY as good as its members.

The same goes for your business. Whether you're hiring employees, engaging contractors, or managing vendors, your team is the backbone of your success.

Building the right team isn't just about finding talent, it's about creating a framework that protects your business, fosters collaboration, and amplifies your message to the world.

Whether your company is just starting out or has hit a Fortune 50 designation, staff can make or break the business each and every day.

Before you bring talent onboard, please invest in a strong legal strategy. Navigating the complexities of employee classification, drafting airtight vendor contracts and maintaining a positive workplace culture, is imperative to your long-term success.

## Why Staff Rocks

Think of your team as the band that brings your business to life. Here's why legal strategy matters:

- **Protects Your Business**: Clear agreements and policies minimize risks like lawsuits, disputes, and compliance penalties.

- **Safeguards Your IP**: Make sure all creative output belongs to your business at creation.

- **Builds a Strong Culture**: Well-defined policies and practices foster trust, transparency, and collaboration.

- **Supports Growth**: Scalable hiring and onboarding processes prepare your business for success.

## From Audition to Hire

Hiring can often feel like a whirlwind, especially when you're eager to grow your business. Most business owners don't realize that cutting corners on employment agreements, policies, or compliance can lead to costly mistakes.

For one, misclassifying employees and contractors is one of the most common pits a company can fall into. Additionally, failing to implement common standards in the workplace can lead to dissatisfaction and disfunction.

As you can see, putting together a great team requires more than just talent, it requires a stable legal foundation.

## How to Form Your Band

### 1. Employee vs. Independent Contractor: Know the Difference

To avoid misclassifying workers here are some basic rules of thumb:

- **Employees:** Are subject to wage laws, tax withholdings and possibly benefits. The company owns all work product.

- **Contractors**: Contractual relationship. No tax withholding or benefits. BUT: Requires clear, written agreements to ensure proper designation and ensure the company owns all work product.

_**Pro Tip**_: Regularly review personnel classifications and audit your agreements to ensure compliance with federal, state, and local laws.

## 2. Clear Agreements

Whether you're hiring employees or engaging contractors, clear agreements are essential.

- **Employment Agreements**: Ascertain the role. Is the person an executive? Entry-level? Somewhere in-between? Will they receive equity? Have you clearly defined job responsibilities, compensation, and reporting structure?

- **Independent Contractor Agreements**: Analyze the role and level of supervision required. Make sure to not let employment concepts bleed into a contractor's role. Regarding expectations, be specific about services required, whether there are deliverables, what the timelines are, and document in writing who owns any resulting work product.

- **Vendor Contracts**: Similar to IC Agreements, Vendor Contracts are often with a company rather than an individual. Whether you are using your own contract or signing theirs, it's important to set expectations.

***Pro Tips***: 1. Operationalize your employment process and stick to it. 2. Train managers who have authority to hire IC's and Vendors to follow this process.

## 3. Protect Your Business with Standard Policies

- **Handbook.** Implement a well-crafted employee handbook as your playbook.

- **Onboarding**: Standardize your onboarding process and include training on corporate policies.

- **Compliance**: Consult with a legal advisor to set anti-harassment, discrimination, and workplace safety policies.

- **Culture**: Have a clear vision that reflects your values and fosters a positive work environment.

***Pro Tip:*** Regularly update your handbook to reflect changes in laws and your business needs.

## 4. Safeguard Your IP and Trade Secrets

The work product produced by your staff is your business's lifeblood, and property. Protect it with:
- **Confidentiality Agreements**: Ensure

sensitive information stays private.

- **IP Assignments**: Ensure all work created by employees or contractors belongs to your business.

- **Trade Secrets:** Trade secret infrastructure will help prevent key team members from taking your secrets to competitors.

***Pro Tip***: Non-competition clauses are illegal in some jurisdictions and frowned upon in others. Make sure you tailor your agreements to your industry and specific jurisdictional risks.

## 5. Plan for the Future

Your team is your greatest asset, invest in their success.

- **Follow the Law**: Employment-related matters are governed by federal, state and local law.

- **Compensation**: Offer competitive salaries, bonuses, and equity incentives.

- **Growth**: Provide opportunities for professional development and advancement, consider implementing ongoing training and education opportunities.

- **Separation**: Handle terminations with care to minimize risks and maintain morale.

***Pro Tip***: Document every step of the hiring, onboarding, and termination process to facilitate good recordkeeping.

## The Final Chord

Building the right team isn't just about finding talent, it's about creating and maintaining a framework that supports your business's growth and protects its future.

# NOTES

DATE: ___________

# 3
# PROTECT YOUR CREATION
## Intellectual Property Essentials

### Four Types of Intellectual Property

INTELLECTUAL PROPERTY OR "IP" are the tools that cement your ownership over what you create, each one plays a distinct role in protecting your business assets.

- **Copyright.** Copyright protects original creative works which are "fixed" in a tangible medium, like writing, recordings, videos, designs, and software.

    - *Example*: The master recordings of a song once it's recorded.

- **Trademark**. Trademark protects brand identifiers, name, logo, tagline, product packaging, and anything that designates a product's source.

- *Example*: A band name and logo.

- **Patent**. Patents protect inventions, systems, and unique technical innovations.

- *Example*: A new kind of effects pedal.

- **Trade Secret**. Protects confidential, valuable information that is not publicly known and not eligible for Copyright, Trademark or Patent protection, like formulas, strategies, or processes.

- *Example*: A process for mixing sound to elicit a certain mood.

As you can see, IP is what sets your company apart. What customers connect with.

*What drives your success.*

IP is the one thing creators, innovators, and entrepreneurs across industries will fight to safeguard.

With the right legal strategy, you'll not only safeguard your IP but unlock its full potential.

## Why IP Rocks

Think of your IP as the hit single that defines your brand.

- **Cements Your Competitive Edge**: Your ideas and creations are what make you unique.

- **Builds Value**: A strong IP portfolio can attract investors, partners, and buyers.

- **Generates Revenue**: Licensing, merchandising, and enforcement can turn your IP into a profit center.

- **Future-Proofs Your Business**: A well-managed IP strategy ensures your assets stay relevant and valuable.

## The Pitfalls of Ignoring IP

I've seen too many businesses, especially in fast-moving industries—overlook or put off focusing on their IP until it's too late.

Do you really want to spend a fortune defending yourself from a competitor who copied your idea from a conference room whiteboard? Or an overseas manufacturer who's counterfeiting your product? Or a competitor deliberately diluting your brand because you never bothered to register your trademarks?

Sure, there's an upfront investment.

The cost of inaction, however, can be devastating.

The truth is, protecting your IP isn't a one-time task. It's an ongoing process that requires strategy, foresight, and expertise.

## The Legal Setlist: Key Moves to Protect Your IP

### 1. Copyrights: Protect Your Creations

Whether it's software, music, films, or games, copyrights safeguard your creative work.

- **Registration**: File for copyright protection to establish ownership.

- **Licensing**: Monetize your work through licensing agreements.

- **Enforcement**: Take action against unauthorized use or infringement.

*__Pro Tip:__* Registering your copyright isn't just a formality, it's your ticket to claiming statutory damages if someone infringes your work. Without registration, you could miss out on significant financial remedies.

## 2. Trademarks: Amplify Your Brand

Your brand is your identity. From the brand name to logos and slogans to the look and feel of your website, trademarks protect what makes you recognizable.

- **Clearance**: Utilize searches and other tools to select available brand.

- **Registration:** Secure your trademarks domestically and internationally.

- **Enforcement**: Monitor for infringement and take action against counterfeiters.

- **Strategy:** Develop a global trademark plan that aligns with your business goals.

*Pro Tip:* Don't just register your trademarks, use them in accordance with your own guidelines to build recognition and value.

## 3. Patents: Secure Your Innovations

If your business relies on technology or unique processes, patents can be incredibly valuable.

- **Registration**: Protect your inventions with

utility or design patents.

- **Strategy**: Build a patent portfolio that supports your long-term goals.

- **Enforcement**: Defend your patents against infringement or challenges.

*__Pro Tip__*: Patents are complex and time-sensitive. Start the process early to avoid missing deadlines.

## 4. Trade Secrets: Stabilize Your Signature Sound

From recipes to algorithms, trade secrets are valuable assets that require careful protection.

- **Policies**: Implement confidentiality agreements, terms of use, and internal safeguards.

- **Monitoring**: Regularly review and update your trade secret protections in agreements.

- **Administration**: Create processes to make sure all your staff follow the rules .

*__Pro Tip__*: Trade secrets cannot be registered, but the right infrastructure can offer long-term protection if managed correctly.

## 5. Application : Defend Your Rights

Stabilizing your IP is about enforcement.

- **Monitoring**: Develop a plan to monitor infringement, counterfeiting, and unauthorized use.

- **Action**: Issue takedown notices, negotiate settlements, or pursue litigation when necessary.

- **Prevention**: Develop policies and guidelines to minimize risks.

   ***Pro Tip***: Always make sure your agreements have strong clauses about your intellectual property rights.

## The Final Chord

Your IP is the heart of your business. Protecting it isn't only about avoiding risks; it's about creating opportunities to expand into global markets and monetize your creations.

# NOTES

*DATE:* _______________

# 4
# SET THE STAGE
## Contracts That Keep Your Business in Sync

A HANDSHAKE DEAL MIGHT feel very rock-and-roll, but it won't likely hold up when the stakes get high.

Contracts aren't just paperwork, they're your backstage pass to smooth partnerships, clear expectations, and long-term success.

Over the years, I've seen too many businesses get burned by vague or overlooked details. Missing provisions. Sloppy drafting. Or, all of the above.

A well-drafted contract isn't just a legal formality; it's a strategic tool to keep your business in sync with partners, clients, and collaborators. Don't scrimp on this step.

### Why Contracts Rock

Think of contracts as a roadmap for a relationship. You don't need to bog it down with unnecessary fluff. In simple terms, you want to describe what you're doing, when things are expected, and how you'll handle the situation if things go off track.

- **Clarity:** Contracts eliminate guesswork by spelling out roles, restrictions, and who's responsible for what.

- **Protection**: Contracts shield your business from uncertainty, providing clarity around disputes, liability, and potential financial losses.

- **Flexibility**: Well-drafted contracts can adapt to changes, ensuring your business stays agile.

- **Trust**: Clear agreements build confidence with partners, investors, and clients.

## The Pitfalls of DIY Contracts

Don't fall into a trap of reusing an old template or downloading some random online form.

While this might seem like a quick, economical solution, the reality is it is unlikely to address the unique needs of your business and can often times create challenging problems. In other words, a one-size-fits-all approach leaves you exposed.

Unfortunately, I say this from a lot of experience. I'm thrust into the role of "fixer" every time a client who tried to cut corners brings me a costly dispute to settle or laments about the opportunities they missed because they signed a bad contract without any legal review without considering the consequences.

Each time, all I can think is "Wow, it's too bad you're just learning that a well-crafted contract is an investment in your business's future."

## Behind the Scenes: Building Agreements That Rock

### 1. Start with the Basics

You should identify, at a minimum:

- **Legal Names of the Parties Involved.**

- **Who's Doing What and By When.**

- **Payment Terms.**

- **Term and Termination.**

- **Intellectual Property Rights Allocation**

- **Liability and Indemnification**

- **Dispute Resolution & Jurisdiction**

- **Confidentiality Terms.**

***Pro Tip***: Don't rely on boilerplate language. Tailor every contract and every provision to your specific needs, whether you're licensing intellectual property, onboarding vendors, or negotiating a co-production deal.

## 2. Protect Your Intellectual Property

As we learned before, IP is one of your company's most valuable asset. Make sure your contracts clearly define:

- **Ownership**: Who owns the rights to the IP.

- **Licensing**: What can partners do with your IP, and for how long.

- **Warranty/Indemnification**: Who's responsible if something goes wrong.

## 3. Anticipate the Unexpected

No one likes to think about worst-case scenarios, but a good agreement includes provisions for:

- **Dispute Resolution**: How will conflicts be handled, mediation, arbitration, or litigation.

- **Force Majeure:** What happens if unforeseen events (like a pandemic) disrupt the agreement.

- **Making Changes**: How can the contract be updated if circumstances change.

## 4. Navigate Industry-Specific Challenges

Every industry has its own quirks, and your contracts should reflect that. Here are a few examples:

- **Gaming and Apps**: User data privacy (COPPA, CCPA, GDPR), monetization policies, and platform compliance (ADA).

- **Entertainment**: Talent agreements, music clearances, and distribution rights.

- **Consumer Products**: Manufacturing, distribution, branding, licensing, and regulatory compliance.

## 5. Think Beyond the Deal

Additional or expanded provisions in an agreement can set your business up for long-term success.

- **Integration Planning**: Consider adding standard processes and approval methods to ensure smooth collaboration with partners and vendors.

- **Ongoing Compliance**: Designate who is

responsible for staying on top of regulatory changes and industry standards.

- **Relationship Management**: By allocating responsibilities, you're able to establish boundaries which, in turn, fosters positive partnerships.

## The Bottom Line

Contracts are the backbone of every successful business relationship. They'll not only protect your interest, they'll create a framework for collaboration, innovation, and growth.

# NOTES

DATE: ___________________

# 5
# OWN THE SPOTLIGHT
## Licensing and Strategic Collaborations

A GREAT SONG WITH little to no airplay can become a global hit when it's licensed for a movie, a commercial, or a video game.

Licensing isn't just about generating revenue, it's about amplifying your message, building your reputation, and creating opportunities you never imagined.

Regardless of your industry, strategic collaborations can take your business to the next level. To do it right, you need more than just a great idea, you need a plan to protect your interest and maximize your impact.

## Why Licensing and Collaborations Rock

Think of licensing as an endless set list to keep your products in the spotlight.

- **Expand Your Reach**: Licensing can put your

brand in front of new audiences and markets.

- **Generate Revenue**: Licensing deals can create new income streams without significant upfront costs.

- **Build Credibility**: Collaborating with established brands or platforms boosts your reputation.

- **Drive Innovation**: Strategic partnerships with companies who can fill in your gaps can lead to opportunities to scale faster.

## The Risks of Going It Alone

Licensing and collaborations are incredibly rewarding, but they also come with risks. Without the right legal framework, you could:

- **Lose Control**: Poorly drafted agreements can dilute your brand or give away too much control over your intellectual property.

- **Face Disputes**: Ambiguous terms can lead to conflicts over royalties, usage rights, or performance.

- **Miss Opportunities**: A lack of strategy can result in deals that don't align with your long-term goals.

All of this is easily avoidable. With the right legal strategies, you can turn these risks into opportunities.

## Key Moves to Own the Spotlight

## 1. Define Your Goals

Before entering into any agreement, ask yourself:
- What do you want to achieve? (e.g., revenue, brand exposure, market expansion)

- Is this an ideal partner? (e.g., a complementary brand, a major platform, a global distributor)

- What are your non-negotiables? (e.g., brand integrity, quality control, exclusivity)

***Pro Tip***: Align your licensing strategy with your overall business goals to ensure consistency and long-term success.

## 2. Protect Your Assets

If you've taken steps to protect your company's valuable assets, don't let a bad deal dilute your hard work.

- **IP Protection**: Ensure your intellectual property is registered and protected in all relevant markets.

- **Quality Control**: Include clauses that allow you to approve how your brand is used.

- **Exclusivity:** Decide whether you want to grant exclusive or non-exclusive rights.

**_Pro Tip_**: Use legal experts who have business experience in your industry to ensure you're heading down the right path.

## 3. Expand Through Strategic Partnerships

Strategic partnerships can open doors to new markets, audiences, and revenue streams. Here's how to make them work:

- **Identify Complementary Brands**: Look for partners whose audience, values, and goals align with yours.

- **Leverage Their Strengths**: Use their

expertise, distribution channels, or technology to amplify your reach.

- **Co-Create Opportunities**: Develop joint products, campaigns, or events that benefit both brands.

***Pro Tip***: Start small with pilot projects to test the partnership before committing to larger initiatives.

## 4. Explore New Opportunities

Licensing isn't just for traditional products, it's about thinking outside the box.

- **Alternative Markets:** License your brand for use in products that are not necessarily in your wheelhouse when there is strategic alignment.

- **Experiential Marketing**: Partner with events, pop-ups, or immersive experiences.

- **Global Reach**: Expand your reach by licensing your product in international markets.

***Pro Tip***: Stay ahead of trends by exploring emerging opportunities in areas like esports, virtual reality, and social commerce.

## 5. Monitor and Enforce

A licensing deal isn't a "set it and forget it" arrangement.

- **Track Performance**: Regularly review sales, royalties, and brand usage to ensure compliance.

- **Address Issues**: Take action if your brand is being misused or if performance targets aren't met.

- **Renew or Revise**: Update agreements to reflect changes in your business or the market.

*__Pro Tip__*: Use technology to streamline tracking, monitoring and reporting, making it easier to manage your relationships

## The Bottom Line

Licensing and strategic collaborations aren't just about making money, they're about creating opportunities to grow your brand, reach new audiences, and stay ahead of the competition.

By approaching these deals with a clear strategy and the right legal framework, you can turn your brand into a global sensation.

# NOTES

DATE: ___________

# 6
# CROWD CONTROL
## Managing Consumer-Facing Legal Risks

WHEN YOU SELL DIRECTLY to consumers, you're not just delivering a product or service, you're building a relationship. And, with that relationship comes responsibility.

From manufacturing to advertising to warranties, every interaction with customers carries legal risks.

This is true whether you're selling physical products, digital services, or something in between. Managing consumer-facing legal risks is essential to protecting your business and maintaining trust.

### Why Consumer Law Rocks

- **Protect Your Business:** Avoid lawsuits, fines, and reputational damage.

- **Build Trust:** Clear policies and fair practices foster customer loyalty.

- **Ensure Compliance:** Stay on the right side of consumer protection laws.

## The Risks of Ignoring Consumer-Facing Legal Issues

It's easy to focus on the excitement of launching a new product or service, but if you and your customers (or clients) are not on the same page, this could lead to disputes and reputational harm.

- **False Advertising or other Consumer Protection Legal Claims:** Misleading marketing can result in lawsuits and fines.

- **Product Liability Issues:** Defective products can lead to injuries and legal action.

- **Privacy and other Regulatory Violations:** Mishandling customer data can damage your reputation and lead to regulatory penalties.

## Key Moves to Manage Consumer-Facing Risks

Your key moves to manage consumer-facing risks are to determine which legal vehicle is most appropriate to address the specific circumstances you face.

Whether it's Terms and Conditions on your website, a SaaS Agreement with one of your customers, or a Consultant Agreement with one of your core clients, having the correct legal vehicle in place will go a long ways towards protecting your specific business.

## 1. Craft Clear Policies

Your policies are the foundation of your customer relationships.

- **Transparent:** Clearly explain your terms of sale, return policies, and warranties.

- **Accessible:** Display your policies prominently on your website and packaging.

- **Fair:** Ensure your policies comply with consumer protection laws and industry standards.

**_Pro Tip_**: Regularly review and update your policies and disclaimer language to reflect changes in laws or your business practices.

## 2. Ensure Product Safety and Compliance

If you're selling physical products, safety and compliance are non-negotiable.

- **Testing and Certification:** Ensure your products meet safety standards and regulations.

- **Labeling:** Provide clear instructions, disclaimers, warnings, and ingredient lists.

- **Recalls:** Have a plan in place to address defects or safety issues quickly.

***Pro Tip***: Work with legal and industry experts to navigate complex regulations, especially if you're selling internationally.

## 3. Protect Customer Data

When you collect customer data, you're responsible for keeping it safe.

- **Privacy Policies:** Clearly explain how you collect, use, and protect customer data.

- **Security Measures:** Use encryption, access controls, and other safeguards to prevent breaches.

- **Compliance:** Stay up-to-date with privacy laws like GDPR, CCPA, and COPPA.

***Pro Tip***: Conduct regular audits to identify and address vulnerabilities in your data practices.

## 4. Manage Advertising and Marketing Risks

Your marketing efforts can attract customers, or lawsuits.

- **Truth in Advertising:** Ensure all claims are accurate, substantiated, and not misleading.

- **Endorsements and Testimonials:** Disclose any paid partnerships or incentives.

- **Promotions:** Comply with laws governing sweepstakes, contests, and discounts.

***Pro Tip***: Train your marketing team on legal requirements to avoid costly mistakes.

## 5. Handle Disputes Professionally

Even the best businesses face customer complaints. Here's how to handle them:

- **Respond Promptly:** Address issues quickly to prevent escalation.

- **Document Everything:** Keep records of customer interactions and resolutions.

- **Offer Solutions:** Be fair and flexible in resolving disputes to maintain trust.

**_Pro Tip_:** Include dispute resolution clauses in your terms of service to encourage mediation or arbitration over litigation.

## The Bottom Line

Selling directly to consumers is an incredible opportunity to build relationships and grow your brand. But it also comes with significant legal risks. By crafting clear policies, ensuring product safety, protecting customer data, and managing advertising risks, you can protect your business and maintain customer trust.

While the challenges may seem daunting, you don't have to face them alone. With the right strategy, you can turn consumer-facing legal risks into opportunities to strengthen your brand and stand out in a competitive market.

# NOTES

DATE: _______________

# 7
# STAY IN HARMONY
## Navigating Privacy Compliance

WE MIGHT AS WELL face it, data is the new currency.

Collecting data means great responsibility. From California to the European Union, governments, consumers, and enterprising litigators are paying closer attention than ever to how businesses collect, use, and protect personal information. Privacy compliance isn't just a legal obligation, it's a critical part of building trust with your customers and staying ahead of the competition.

Privacy laws like GDPR, CCPA, and COPPA are no longer optional. They're the rules of the road for doing business in a data-driven world. And while the regulations can feel overwhelming, they're also an opportunity to show your customers you value their trust.

## Why Privacy Rocks

Think of privacy compliance as the soundcheck before a big show. It's not the most glamorous part of the process, but it's what ensures everything runs smoothly.

- **Build Trust:** Clear privacy policies show customers you value their data.

- **Avoid Potential Fines:** Non-compliance can lead to hefty penalties and legal headaches.

- **Protect Your Reputation:** A data breach or privacy scandal is a PR nightmare and will damage your reputation.

- **Support Growth:** A strong privacy strategy prepares your business for global markets.

## The Risks of Ignoring Privacy Compliance

It's easy to put privacy on the back burner, especially when you're focused on growth, customer acquisition and sales. But the consequences of non-compliance can derail everything you've worked hard for. Investing into your privacy compliance now will help you avoid reputational damage which could take years to repair.

The good news? Privacy compliance doesn't have to be a burden. With the right strategy, you can turn it into a competitive advantage.

# Key Moves to Stay in Harmony

## 1. Know the Rules

Privacy laws vary by region and industry. Here is a simple cheat sheet:

- **GDPR:** The European Union's strict data protection law applies to any business handling EU residents' data (*hint*: if you operate a website, you're global).

- **CCPA:** California's privacy law gives consumers control over their personal information.

- **COPPA:** Protects children's data for businesses targeting users under 13.

- **TCPA:** Regulates telemarketing and text messaging.

  ***Pro Tip***: Don't assume compliance with one law means you're covered for all. Each regulation has its own nuances, and you must solve for the lowest common denominator.

## 2. Craft Clear Privacy Policies

Your privacy policy is your first line of defense. Make sure it's:

- **Transparent:** Clearly explain what data you collect, how you use it, and who you share it with.

- **Accessible:** Make your policy easy to find and understand.

- **Customized:** Avoid generic templates, your policy should reflect your unique business practices and data collection realities.

   **_Pro Tip_:** Copying someone else's privacy policy is WORSE than having no policy at all. Your technology and collection methods might differ and the key to compliance is transparency and accuracy.

## 3. Implement Privacy-by-Design

Privacy shouldn't be an afterthought, it should be built into your products and processes.

- **Data Minimization:** Only collect and store the data you need and make sure to include your legal team into the product development cycle at every stage.

- **Security Measures:** Use encryption, access controls, and other safeguards to protect data.

- **User Control:** Give customers clear options to manage their data, like opt-out and/or deletion requests.

***Pro Tip*:** Conduct regular privacy impact assessments to identify and address risks.

## 4. Train Your Team

Your employees are your first line of defense. Make sure they understand:

- **Data Handling:** How to collect, store, and share data in accordance with your policy; update your privacy policy if your business processes change.

- **Compliance Requirements:** Privacy rules and regulations are changing constantly, this is not a "one and done" situation.

- **Breach Response:** Have a plan in place in case something goes wrong.

***Pro Tip*:** Regular education and training will keep your team prepared for new challenges.

## 5. Plan for the Worst

Even the best-prepared businesses can face data breaches or regulatory investigations. Be ready with:

- **Incident Response Plans:** Work with your legal team to develop data breach protocol.

- **Documentation:** Keep records of your compliance efforts to show regulators if the situation arises. Your good-faith efforts mean something!

- **Legal Support:** Make sure you're working with a legal team that knows how to handle privacy disputes and investigations.

**_Pro Tip_:** Test your incident response plan on a regular basis to ensure it works.

## The Bottom Line

Privacy compliance isn't only about avoiding fines or lawsuits, it's about building a business that customers trust. In a world where data breaches make headlines and consumers are more aware of their rights than ever, a strong privacy strategy can set you apart from the competition.

While the rules may seem daunting, you don't have to navigate them alone. With the right guidance, you can turn privacy compliance into a strength, and keep your business in harmony with the law.

# NOTES

DATE: ___________

# 8
# SHIELD THE STAGE

## Risk Management to Avoid Legal Blowouts

A BLOWN SPEAKER OR a broken guitar string can derail even the most stellar player's performance.

In business, the stakes are even higher. From contract disputes to data breaches, legal risks can disrupt your operations, damage your reputation, and drain your bank account.

Risk management isn't just a safety net, it's a strategic tool to keep your business running smoothly.

When you realistically identify potential pitfalls, you can put the right operational safeguards in place. Now you can focus on what you do best: creating something extraordinary.

### Why Risk Management Rocks:

Think of risk management as the tour manager who ensures each show goes off without a hitch.

- **Protect Your Assets:** Safeguard your business from lawsuits, fines, and other liabilities.

- **Build Confidence:** Investors, partners, and customers trust businesses that manage risk effectively.

- **Support Growth:** A strong risk management strategy prepares your business for new opportunities.

- **Minimize Disruptions:** Proactive planning keeps your business running smoothly even when challenges arise.

## The Hazards of Ignoring Risk Management

I never understand why business owners put risk management on the back burner and prefer to solve problems as they arise; it reminds me of burying your head in the sand. I've seen first-hand how the consequences of inaction can be severe. Lawsuits, regulatory penalties, and reputational damage are not fun and pull your focus away from day to day operations and put a drain on working capital.

The good news? Risk management doesn't have to be overwhelming. With the right implementation of strategy, you can turn potential threats into opportunities for growth.

## Key Moves to Shield Your Business

### 1. Identify Risks

It may seem simple, but every business faces their own unique risks. Start by asking:

- **What are your biggest liabilities?** (e.g., contracts, intellectual property, data privacy)

- **Where are you most vulnerable?** (e.g., regulatory compliance, employee disputes)

- **How could risks disrupt your operations?** (e.g., supply chain issues, cyberattacks)

*Pro Tip*: Conduct regular risk assessments with your executive team to stay ahead of potential threats.

### 2. Optimize Operational Processes

Efficient operations are the backbone of a successful business, but they're also a common source of risk.

- **Standardize Policies and Procedures:** Create clear, written procedures for your processes to ensure consistency and compliance like "SOPs" or "Standard Operating Procedures." Create company-wide policies (like PTO, Workplace Etiquette, contract signatory authority, etc.). Make these available to all staff via your preferred communication method.

- **Train Your Team:** Once procedures are documented, educate and train staff on best practices and risk management protocols. Incorporate into your onboarding processes for new team members.

- **Monitor Compliance:** Regularly review your operations to identify and address potential risks, implement new policies as the need arises.

   ***Pro Tip***: Use technology to automate and streamline your processes, reducing the risk of human error or miscommunication.

## 3. Manage Relationships

Relationships are the backbone of every business, but they're also a common source of disputes.

- **Draft Clear Agreements:** Any person or company who has a relationship with your company should be subject to some written agreement to define roles, responsibilities, and expectations.

- **Monitor Compliance:** Ensure you hold everyone accountable in meeting their obligations to your company.

- **Plan for Disputes:** Include standard dispute resolution clauses to handle conflicts efficiently.

_**Pro Tip**_: Regularly review and update your contracts to reflect changes in your business or the law, amend agreements when necessary.

## 4. Prepare for the Unexpected

Even the best-prepared businesses can face unexpected challenges. Be ready with:

- **Insurance:** Protect your business with policies that cover key risks, like liability, property damage, and cyberattacks.

- **Crisis Management Plans:** Develop protocols for handling emergencies, from data breaches to PR issues.

- **Legal Support:** Work with a team that has a business and operational background, they'll know how to navigate complex legal issues and disputes in a way that jives with your business objectives and won't lead you down a litigation rabbit hole.

**_Pro Tip_**: Audit and test your crisis management plans at least once every year to ensure they work when you need them.

## The Bottom Line

Risk management is mostly about creating a business that's resilient, adaptable, and ready for whatever comes its way. By identifying potential risks and putting the right safeguards in place, you can protect your assets, build trust with stakeholders, and focus on what you do best: growing your business.

# NOTES

*DATE:* ___________

# 9
# AVOID FEEDBACK

## Smart Dispute Resolution Strategies

UNLESS YOU'RE AT A 90's grunge concert, feedback from a microphone or a speaker will ruin your night.

In business, legal disputes will have the same effect not only by derailing your operations, but by damaging relationships and causing you to lose precious time and money.

The good news is, not every disagreement has to end in a legal battle. With the right mindset, you can resolve conflicts efficiently outside of court.

My philosophy is simple: avoid litigation whenever possible. But when disputes are unavoidable, don't treat them as a cost center, treat them as an opportunity to protect your business and strengthen your relationships.

### Why Smart Dispute Resolution Rocks

- **Save Time and Money:** Litigation is

expensive and time-consuming and can drag out for years.

- **Preserve Relationships:** Resolving disputes amicably keeps partnerships intact and maintains trust.

- **Protect Your Reputation:** Avoiding public legal battles helps you maintain a positive image both internally and externally.

- **Keep You in Control:** Proactive resolution puts you in the driver's seat, rather than leaving outcomes to a judge or jury who may not understand your business.

## The Risks of Ignoring Disputes

It's tempting to hope that disputes will resolve themselves, but that's rarely the case. Ignoring conflicts can lead to:

- **Escalation:** Small disagreements can snowball into major legal battles or judgements against you.

- **Financial Losses:** Litigation can drain your resources and disrupt your operations.

- **Damaged Relationships:** Unresolved

disputes can sour partnerships and harm your reputation.

## Key Moves to Resolve Disputes

## 1. Act with Integrity and Respect

How you handle conflicts sets the tone for resolution.

- **Be Courteous:** Treat everyone involved (including your adversary) with respect, from emails to formal letters, even if tensions are high. Once you're in conflict, every aspect of your communication might be judged, and you want to always take the high road.

- **Be Honest:** Transparency builds trust and can prevent misunderstandings from escalating. If your company is in the wrong, figure out a way to make things right if possible. If your company has been wronged, try to keep a cool head and identify what you need to resolve the issue.

- **Be Proactive:** Address issues head-on before they spiral out of control.

***Pro Tip***: A simple, respectful conversation can often resolve conflicts before they require legal intervention.

## 2. Draft Clear Contracts

A well-drafted conflict resolution process in your contracts can help prevent disputes before they start.

- **Define Terms:** Use precise language and clear escalation processes to avoid ambiguity.

- **Conflict Process:** Specify how conflicts will be handled, whether through mediation, arbitration, or litigation.

- **Work With Your Attorney:** Always have a legal expert review your contracts to help devise your strategy.

***Pro Tip***: Regularly update your contracts to reflect changes in your business or the law.

## 3. Document Everything

Keeping clear and contemporaneous records are your best defense in any dispute.

- **Contracts:** Follow the dispute resolution process in your agreement, paying attention to breach clauses.

- **Communications:** Keep records of texts, emails, meeting notes, chats, and other correspondence related to the dispute.

- **Evidence:** Gather photos, receipts, or other documentation that supports your position.

*__Pro Tip__*: Develop a company-wide system to keep records organized and accessible.

## 4. Understand the Difference: Litigation vs. Alternative Dispute Resolution (ADR)

Litigation isn't the only option when disputes arise. Alternative Dispute Resolution (ADR) methods like mediation and arbitration *may* offer more flexibility and control over the process.

However, they're not always faster, cheaper, or less adversarial than court, it depends on the situation. Here's a breakdown of each option:

## Mediation: Finding Common Ground

Mediation involves a neutral third party (the mediator) who helps both sides negotiate a resolution. The mediator doesn't make decisions but facilitates communication and guides the parties toward a mutually acceptable solution.

## 1. Pros of Mediation

- **Collaborative:** Encourages open dialogue and creative problem-solving.

- **Less Invasive:** Discovery is limited and so is testimony.

- **Confidential:** Mediation is private, unlike court proceedings, which are public.

- **Cost-Effective:** Typically much less expensive than litigation or arbitration.

- **Faster:** Can resolve disputes in days or weeks, rather than months or years.

## 2. Cons of Mediation

- **Non-Binding:** If an agreement isn't reached by the end of the mediation, the dispute may still end up in court.

- **Requires Cooperation:** Both parties must be willing to negotiate in good faith in accordance with the dispute process in the Agreement.

- **Limited Enforcement:** Remedies are only

enforceable if both parties sign an agreement following the mediation.

## 3. When to Use Mediation

- You want to preserve a business relationship.

- It's required under the contract.

- You're looking for a creative, flexible solution.

- Mediation makes sense for the remedy you seek.

## Arbitration: A Private Courtroom

Arbitration involves a neutral third party (the arbitrator) who acts like a private judge, hearing evidence and making a binding decision. It's often used when contracts include arbitration clauses.

## 1. Pros of Arbitration

- **Private:** Unlike court cases, arbitration is confidential.

- **Flexible:** Parties can choose the arbitrator (often with experience in their particular industry) and tailor the process to their needs.

- **Final:** Arbitration awards are binding and enforceable in court. Most jurisdictions will not allow appeals.

- **Potentially Faster:** Can be quicker than litigation, depending on the complexity of the case.

## 2. Cons of Arbitration

- **Cost:** Arbitration can be more expensive than going to court because you pay an hourly rate for the arbitrator and venue, and still incur other litigation expenses like discovery and expert witnesses.

- **Limited Appeal:** Arbitration awards are difficult to challenge, even if there's an error in the decision.

- **Adversarial:** While less formal than court, arbitration can still feel confrontational.

- **Unpredictable:** Arbitrators have broad discretion, which can lead to extraordinarily inconsistent outcomes that do not always follow legal precedent.

## 3. When to Use Arbitration

- You want a binding decision without going to court.

- The dispute involves technical or industry-specific issues (e.g., intellectual property, construction) and you're able to choose an arbitrator with expertise in this area.

- Your contract requires it.

## Litigation: The Traditional Route

Litigation involves taking your dispute to court, where a judge (and sometimes a jury) makes a legally binding decision.

## 1. Pros of Litigation

- **Formal Process:** Clear rules and procedures govern the process and you can rely on legal precedent.

- **Appeals:** If you disagree with the outcome, you can appeal the decision.

- **Enforceable:** Court judgments are backed by the full force of the law.

- **Transparent:** Public proceedings can provide accountability.

## 2. Cons of Litigation

- **Expensive:** Legal fees, court costs, and expert witnesses can add up quickly.

- **Time-Consuming:** Cases can take months or even years to resolve.

- **Adversarial:** The process can strain relationships and damage reputations and take focus away from your day to day operations. Not to mention the toll it takes on your mental health.

- **Public:** Court cases are part of the public record, which can be a disadvantage for businesses.

## 3. When to Use Litigation

- The dispute involves significant legal or factual issues that require a formal ruling.

- The amount in controversy is substantial and you don't want to risk arbitration.

- You need a legally enforceable decision.

- ADR methods have failed to resolve the dispute.

## Choosing the Right Path

The best dispute resolution method depends on your specific situation. Here's a quick guide:

- **Mediation:** Use when you want to preserve relationships and explore creative solutions.

- **Arbitration:** Use when you need a binding decision but want to avoid the public nature of court.

- **Litigation:** Use when the stakes are high, and you need a formal, enforceable ruling.

**_Pro Tip_:** Include strategic litigation clauses in your contracts to encourage your preferred method of resolution and keep the jurisdiction to where your company is located.

## Be Prepared to Pivot:

Sometimes, disputes can't be resolved amicably.

When this happens:

- **Consult Your Attorney:** A legal expert can help you assess your options and develop a strategy and ensure you have a shield of attorney/client privilege protection.

- **Stay Professional:** Keep emotions in check and focus on protecting your business.

- **Be Prepared:** Gather all relevant documentation and evidence to support your case.

**_Pro Tip_**: Even in litigation, look for opportunities to settle out of court to save time and resources.

## The Bottom Line:

Disputes are inevitable in business, how you handle them makes all the difference. While litigation is sometimes unavoidable, it doesn't have to be a never-ending cost center.

With the right strategy, you can turn disputes into opportunities to protect your business and strengthen your relationships.

# NOTES

DATE: ______________

# 10
# When the Show Must Go On

## Scaling and Growing Your Business

GRADUATING FROM SMALL GIGS to sold-out arenas requires more than just talent, it takes strategy, planning, and the ability to adapt to challenges.

Growth doesn't happen by accident. It requires a clear vision, a stable legal foundation, and the ability to navigate obstacles along the way. Here's how to scale your business like a rockstar, and keep the show going, no matter what.

### Why Scaling Rocks

Think of scaling as your encore, the moment when your hard work pays off and your business reaches new heights.

- **Expand Your Reach:** Growth opens doors to new markets, customers, and revenue streams.

- **Build Credibility:** A scalable business attracts investors, partners, and top talent.

- **Drive Innovation:** Scaling forces you to implement strategies to stay ahead of the competition.

- **Create Legacy:** A well-scaled business can outlast its founders and make a lasting impact.

## The Risks of Scaling Without a Plan

Scaling is exciting, but it's not without risks. I've worked with businesses that grew too fast, only to face:

- **Operational Chaos:** Inefficient processes can't keep up with demand.

- **Legal Pitfalls:** Ignoring compliance or IP issues can lead to costly disputes.

- **Financial Strain:** Rapid growth can drain resources if not managed carefully.

- **Cultural Erosion:** Losing your company culture can alienate employees and customers.

The good news? With the right strategies, you can scale your business while minimizing risks.

## Key Moves to Scale Like a Pro

## 1. Regularly Review and Adjust Your Business

Scaling your business isn't a one-time effort, it's an ongoing process that requires constant attention to your foundation. Think of it like tuning your instrument before every performance: regular maintenance ensures you're always ready to hit the right notes.

Here's how to keep your business strong and scalable:

- **Monitor Your IP:** Regularly check for unauthorized use of your trademarks, copyrights, or patents.

- **Update Registrations:** Ensure your IP protections are current and cover new products, services, or markets.

- **Implement Scalable Operational Procedures**: Train your team on your SOP's and Policies?.

- **Hiring and Onboarding:** Develop standardized procedures for recruiting, training, and integrating new team members.

- **Customer Service:** Create scalable systems to handle increased demand without sacrificing quality.

- **Technology:** Invest in tools like CRM software, automation platforms, and project management systems to streamline workflows.

***Pro Tip:*** Be objective and identify bottlenecks to improve scalability.

## 2. Secure Funding for Growth

Scaling requires resources. Explore funding options like:

- **Investment:** Attract venture capital or angel investors with a compelling pitch and stable business plan.

- **Loans:** Secure business loans or lines of credit to finance expansion.

- **Crowdfunding:** Use platforms like Kickstarter or Indiegogo to raise funds and build a loyal customer base.

***Pro Tip***: Work with legal experts to draft investor agreements and ensure compliance with securities laws.

## 3. Expand Your Market Reach

Growth often means entering new markets. Here's how to do it successfully:

- **Research:** Understand the demographics, regulations, and competition in your target market.

- **Localize:** Adapt your products, services, and marketing to resonate with local audiences.

- **Collaborate:** Collaborate with local businesses or distributors to accelerate your entry.

***Pro Tip***: Protect your brand by registering trademarks in expanded markets.

## 4. Innovate and Diversify

Scaling is not about doing more it's about doing better.

- **New Products:** Expand your offerings to meet evolving customer needs.

- **Technology:** Invest in tools and platforms

that streamline operations and enhance customer experiences.

- **Partnerships:** Identify other businesses who have created products and services that could enhance your own offerings and work together.

***Pro Tip:*** Use customer feedback to guide your innovation efforts and ensure your products resonate.

## 5. Manage Risks Along the Way

Growth brings new risks. Stay ahead by:

- **Compliance:** Ensure your business meets all legal and regulatory requirements in new markets.

- **Crisis Planning:** Develop protocols for handling emergencies, from data breaches to PR crises.

- **Culture Preservation:** Maintain your company's core values as you grow to keep employees and customers engaged.

***Pro Tip:*** Regularly assess your risk management strategies and update them as your business evolves.

## The Bottom Line

Scaling your business is one of the most exciting, and challenging phases of entrepreneurship. While the journey may have its ups and downs, with the right strategy and support, you can scale your business like a rockstar and keep the tour going for years to come.

# NOTES

*DATE:* _______________

# 11
# ENCORE

Every great performance deserves one last song, a powerful finish to leave the audience inspired and wanting more.

You're ready to put in the work. Stabilize the stage. Protect what matters. Amplify your impact.

Now it's time to keep the momentum going.

The tools and tactics in this book are your first setlist, the foundational moves to stabilize, amplify, protect, and grow what you're building.

They don't replace having the right team on the road with you, tuning the mix and managing the chaos behind the curtain. That's where the right legal partner comes in.

If you're ready to level up, take it from the garage to the arena, and build something with real staying power, stick around for the next chapter. We'd love to show you how we help businesses like yours rock, every single day.

# NOTES

*DATE:* _______________

# 12
# FINAL ENCORE
## Why Your Business Needs Lawyers Who Rock

STARTING AND GROWING YOUR business is an exhilarating journey, but it's also filled with challenges. From navigating complex regulations to protecting your intellectual property, managing risks, and forging strategic partnerships, the legal landscape can feel like a minefield.

That's why having a lawyer who truly understands business isn't just helpful, it's essential.

At HMLG, we don't just provide legal advice; we provide business solutions with an exceptional combination of legal expertise and real-world business experience.

We work closely with clients across industries, gaming, technology, consumer products, media, and more helping them navigate every stage of business, from formation and operations to fundraising, licensing, and strategic partnerships.

## Why HMLG is Different

Here's how we stand apart:

## 1. We Understand Your Business

We're not just lawyers,, we're business people. Our team has served as in-house counsel, business executives, strategic advisors, and board members. We know how to align legal strategy with your business goals, ensuring that every decision supports your growth and success.

## 2. We're Proactive, Not Reactive

We don't wait for problems to arise. We anticipate risks, identify opportunities, and provide actionable advice to keep your business on track. Whether it's drafting contracts, managing compliance, or navigating disputes, we're always one step ahead.

## 3. We're Collaborative and Accessible

At HMLG, we're not just your lawyers, we're your C-suite level strategic advisors. We work closely with your executives or existing in-house counsel to understand your challenges, goals, and vision. Whether you need help with a one-time project or ongoing legal support, we're here to make your success our top priority.

## 4. We Bring a Creative, Forward-Thinking Approach

Our slogan, *Your Lawyers Should Rock®*, reflects how we think, creative, innovative, and client-focused. We don't just follow trends; we help set them. From licensing and intellectual property to digital media and consumer products, we bring a fresh perspective to every challenge.

## 5. We're Certified and Committed

HMLG is certified as a Women's Business Enterprise by the Women's Business Enterprise National Council (WBENC), the nation's largest third-party certifier of businesses owned and operated by women. We're proud to bring diversity, expertise, and a commitment to excellence to every client relationship.

## Your Next Move

Your business is more than just a company, it's your legacy. You need a legal team that understands your vision and has the expertise to make it a reality.

At HMLG, we're here to help you **stabilize, protect, and amplify** your business and provide the legal foundation you need to thrive.

Ready to take your business to the next level?

Let's talk. Because when it comes to your business, you don't just need any old lawyer, you need **Lawyers Who ROCK!**

***

Leave a review here: Amazon

Follow me everywhere.

For special announcements and updates click here.

# NOTES

DATE: ____________

# About the Author

Joleen Winther Hughes founded Hughes Media Law Group to give creators, founders, and growing businesses the kind of legal support most firms don't offer. Practical. Strategic. Grounded in how businesses actually operate. HMLG helps clients stabilize their foundation, protect what matters, and amplify growth without killing momentum.

Her approach comes from real-world experience, not theory, and from a core belief simple in concept and powerful in practice. Legal strategy should fuel growth, not slow it down.

Joleen has long supported creative and innovative communities through leadership and service, including prior work as Music Commissioner for the City of Seattle and executive board service with Seattle International Film Festival. Her podcast, The Lawyer Who Rocks, returns in 2026, continuing conversations about law, business, and creativity without the usual legal jargon. She also has a secret career as  a best-selling romance author under a pseudonym.

# ABOUT THE FIRM

Hughes Media Law Group combines legal expertise with real-world business experience, providing creative, forward-thinking solutions that help businesses stabilize, protect, and amplify their success.

With a focus on industries like gaming, tech, media, and consumer facing products, HMLG works with startups and established companies to deliver strategic in-house level legal guidance tailored to their goals.

From entity formation and intellectual property protection to licensing and risk management, HMLG is dedicated to helping businesses build a strong foundation for growth.

At HMLG, our belief is simple: **Your Lawyers Should Rock** ®

# Acknowledgements

This book would not exist without the incredible people who supported, inspired, and challenged me along the way.

To my husband, who encouraged me to take the leap and start my own firm when it was only a dream. Your belief in me gave me the courage to build something new.

To my dad, whose stories of his own legal practice sparked my passion at a young age to use the law as a way to help others. Your example set the course for everything I do.

To the extraordinary team at Hughes Media Law Group—past and present. Thank you for your hard work, dedication, and willingness to embrace and elevate my vision. You are the reason this firm has become what it is, and I am endlessly appreciative for your trust and talent.

To the Seattle music community, which has been my home and inspiration for nearly four decades. I am proud and honored to be part of such a creative, bold, and fiercely independent collective of artists and entrepreneurs.

To RealNetworks, the company that invented streaming media, and my treasured colleagues there. I am grateful for your trust and the opportunities I had to grow, learn, and contribute to something that changed history. My success would not have been possible without the foundation I built alongside you.

To my mentors, Susan and KellyJo. It is rare to have one strong, kind, supportive female role model, let alone two. Your collective wisdom, encouragement, and example guide me daily. I hear your voices reminding me what truly matters in leadership and life.

To the clients I've had the privilege to work with over the years—thank you for trusting me with your businesses, challenges, and dreams. You've taught me as much as I've advised you, and I'm honored to be part of your journeys.

# NOTES

DATE: _____________

# NOTES

DATE: ___________

# NOTES

DATE: _______________

# NOTES

DATE: ______________